MY FIRST REPTILES & AMPHIBIANS ENCYCLOPEDIA

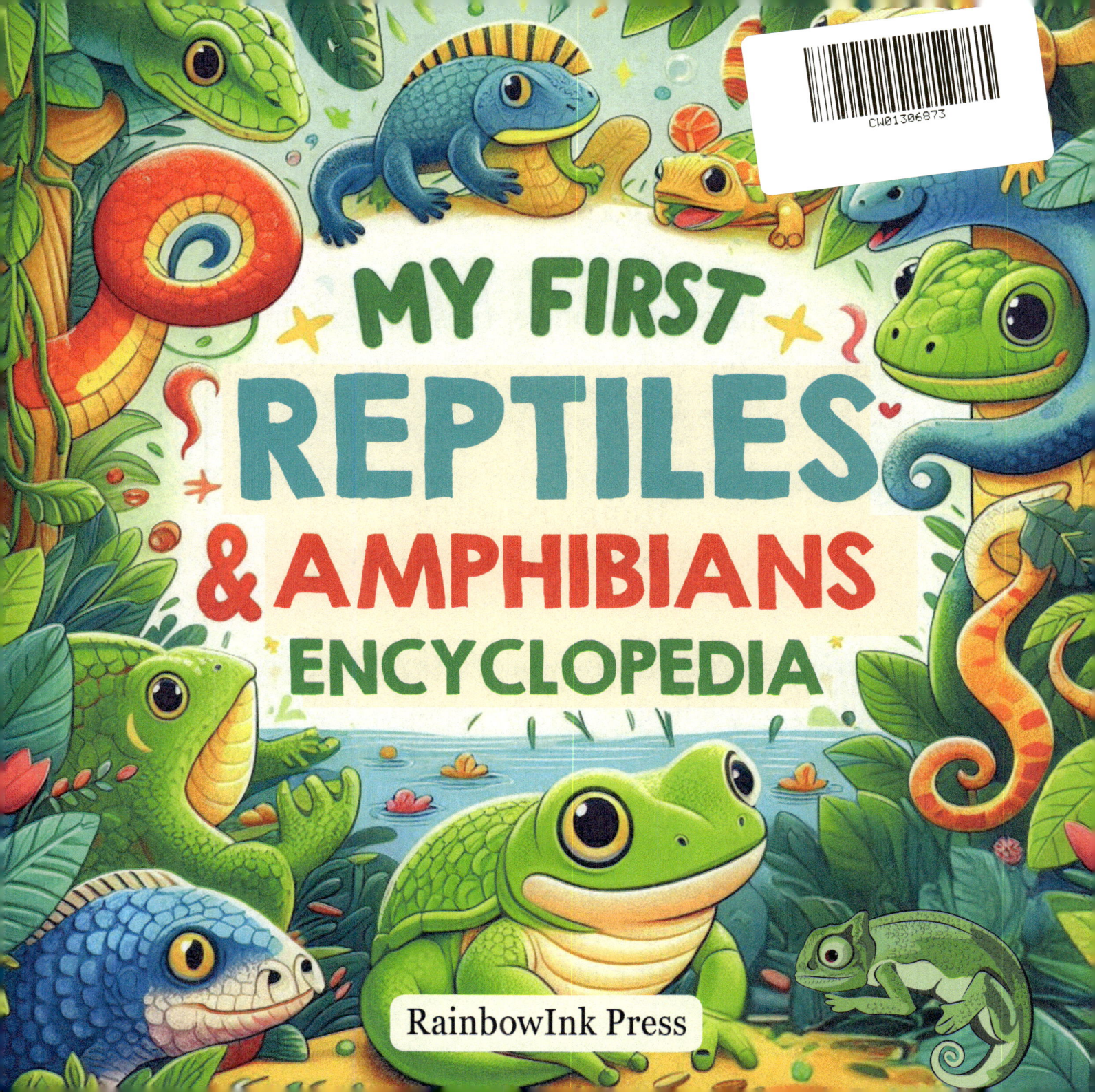

RainbowInk Press

WELCOME TO THE ADVENTURE!

OUR DEAREST READERS,

Welcome to a world of amazing reptiles and amphibians! Dive in, explore, and have fun discovering these incredible creatures. Let your curiosity lead the way!

**Happy Reading,
RAINBOWINK PRESS** 🌈

Copyright © 2024 Rainbowink Press All rights reserved. No part of this publication may be reproduced, distributed, or transmitted in any form or by any means, including photocopying, recording, or other electronic or mechanical methods, without the prior written permission of the publisher, except in the case of brief quotations embodied in critical reviews and certain other noncommercial uses permitted by copyright law. For permission requests, please contact Rainbowink Press.

TABLE OF CONTENTS

- **INTRODUCTION** 5
- **REPTILES** 9
- **Galápagos Tortoise** 13
- **Green Iguana** 19
- **King Cobra** 25
- **Komodo Dragon** 31
- **Leopard Gecko** 37
- **AMPHIBIANS** 43
- **African Bullfrog** 47
- **Axolotl** 53
- **Poison Dart Frog** 59
- **Red-Eyed Tree Frog** 65
- **Tiger Salamander** 71
- **TIPS AND TEACHINGS** 77

4.

INTRODUCTION

HELLO, YOUNG EXPLORERS! 🌟

We're so excited that you've picked up this book! 🥳 At RainbowInk Press, we love creating fun and colorful books just for kids like you. In this encyclopedia, you'll jump into the amazing world of reptiles and amphibians. 🦎🐍

What Are Reptiles and Amphibians? 🤔

Reptiles are cool creatures with scaly skin, like snakes, lizards, and turtles. 🦎 They usually lay eggs and love to sunbathe to stay warm. Amphibians, like frogs and salamanders, are animals that live both in water and on land. 🐸 They have smooth, moist skin and can breathe through it, too!

Why Are They Special? ✨

These animals have been around for millions of years—long before even the dinosaurs disappeared! They come in all shapes, sizes, and colors, and each one has a special role in nature. 🌍

What Will You Discover? 🕵️

In this book, you'll meet 10 amazing reptiles and amphibians. You'll learn where they live, what they eat, and some super cool facts that will make you say, "Wow!" 😮

Let's Get Started! 🚀

Grab your explorer's hat 🎩 and get ready to dive into a world full of scaly, slimy, and totally awesome creatures. Who knows? Maybe one day you'll discover a new reptile or amphibian that no one has ever seen before! 🌈

Happy reading and exploring! 🥳

Your friends at RainbowInk Press 🌈

8.

REPTILES
THE SCALY SUPERSTARS!

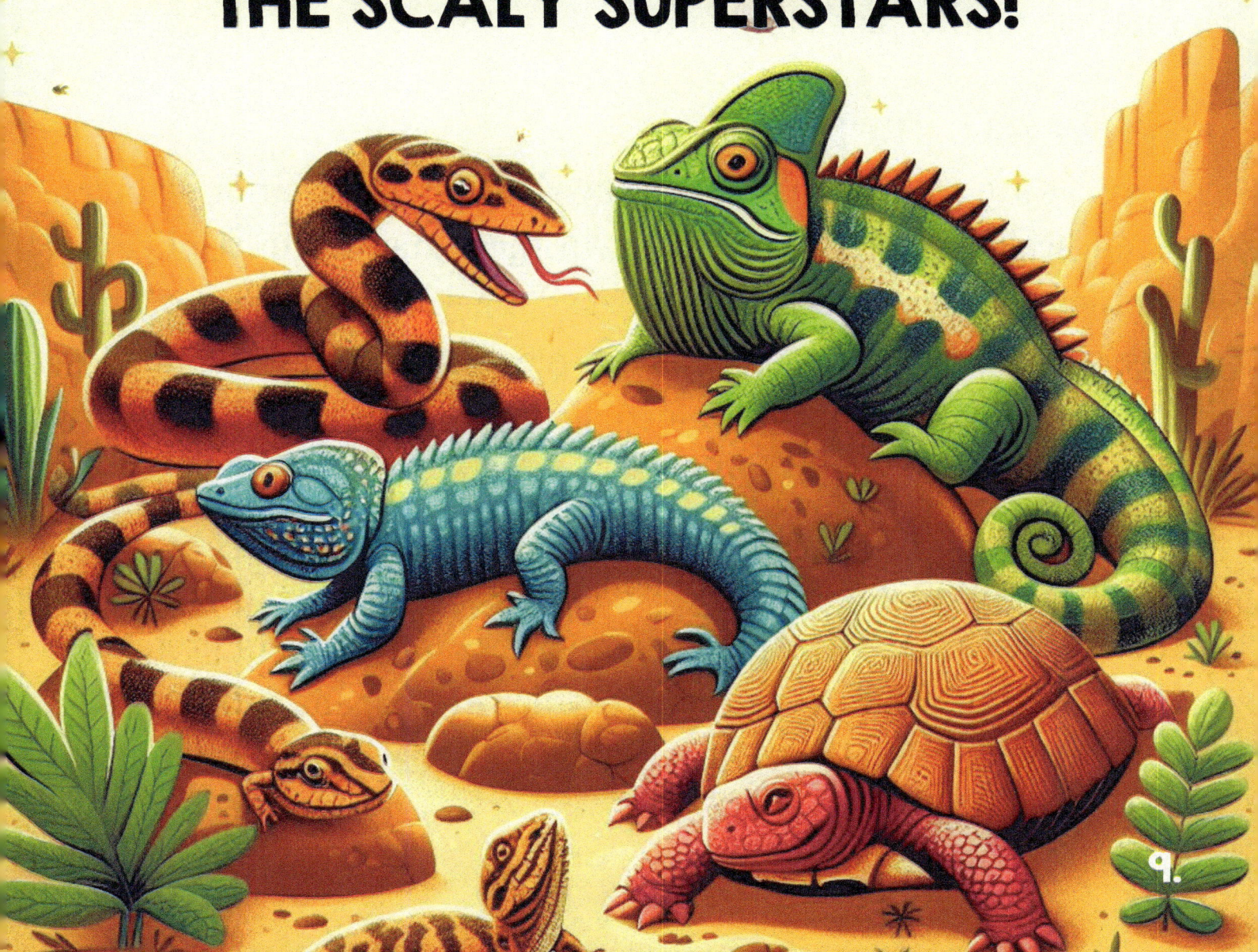

Reptiles are some of the coolest creatures on Earth! They come in all shapes and sizes, from tiny lizards that can fit in your hand to giant tortoises that weigh more than you! But what makes a reptile a reptile? Let's find out!

WHAT ARE REPTILES?

Reptiles are animals that have scaly skin instead of fur or feathers. Their scales protect them and help them stay warm. Unlike us, reptiles don't have to eat every day! They can go days, or even weeks, without eating after a big meal. And guess what? Most reptiles hatch from eggs laid by their mothers.

WHERE DO REPTILES LIVE?

Reptiles can be found almost everywhere on Earth! Some live in the deserts, where it's super hot and dry, while others prefer the cool shade of rainforests. Some reptiles even spend most of their time in water, like crocodiles! Wherever they are, reptiles have special skills that help them survive.

COLD-BLOODED? WHAT DOES THAT MEAN?

Reptiles are cold-blooded, which means they can't make their own body heat. Instead, they warm up by basking in the sun or cool down by hiding in the shade. That's why you might see lizards soaking up the sun on a rock—they're getting their energy!

12.

GALÁPAGOS TORTOISE:

13.

BASIC CHARACTERISTICS :

Scientific Name: Chelonoidis nigra

Size: The Galápagos tortoise is one of the largest tortoises in the world, growing up to 4 to 5 feet long and weighing up to 500 pounds!

Color: They have a brown or gray shell (called a carapace) that is shaped like a dome, and their skin is rough and leathery.

WHERE DO THEY LIVE?

Galápagos tortoises are native to the Galápagos Islands, located off the coast of Ecuador in South America. These islands are volcanic and full of unique wildlife, including the giant tortoise. They prefer dry, grassy areas but can also be found in humid highlands. They move slowly and can travel long distances to find food.

WHAT DO THEY EAT?

Galápagos tortoises are herbivores, meaning they eat only plants. Their diet mainly consists of grasses, leaves, fruits, and cactus pads.

These tortoises can survive long periods without food or water, thanks to the water stored in their bodies and their slow metabolism.

SPECIAL ABILITIES :

Long Lifespan: Galápagos tortoises can live over 100 years, with some even reaching 150 years old, making them one of the longest-living animals on the planet.

Water Storage: They can store water in their bodies for months, which helps them survive in dry conditions.

Slow and Steady: Though they move slowly (around 0.3 mph), they can travel up to 8 miles in a day in search of food and water.

16.

FUN FACTS :

Shell Shape: Different species of Galápagos tortoises have different shell shapes. Tortoises living in dry areas have "saddleback" shells, while those in humid areas have "domed" shells.

Historical Importance: Galápagos tortoises were once studied by Charles Darwin, helping him develop his famous theory of evolution.

Gentle Giants: Despite their enormous size, Galápagos tortoises are peaceful creatures, spending most of their day resting, basking in the sun, or slowly munching on plants.

Galápagos tortoises are true island giants, with a fascinating history and incredible ability to adapt to their environment, making them one of nature's most impressive reptiles!

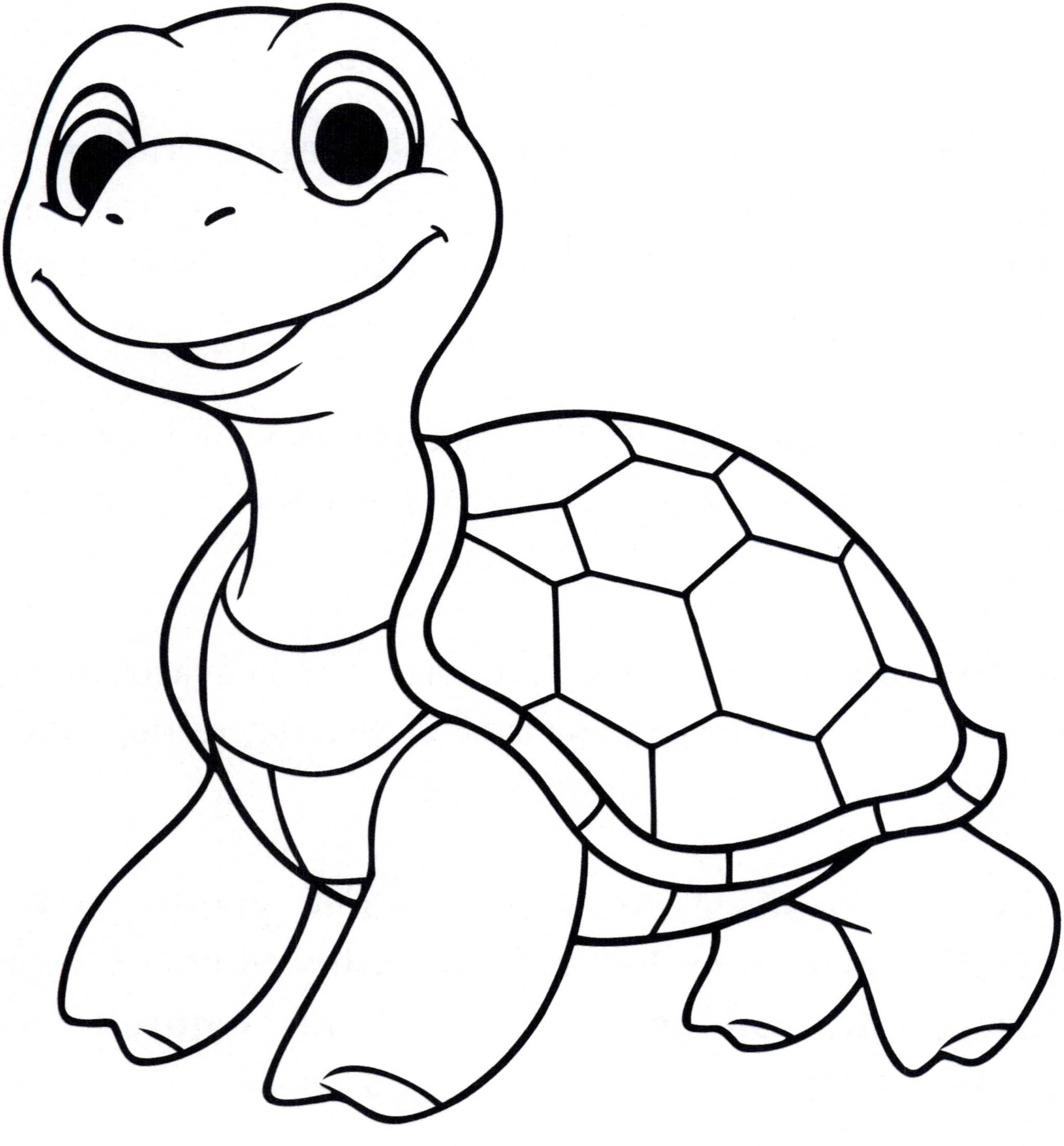

GREEN IGUANA

BASIC CHARACTERISTICS :

Scientific Name: Iguana iguana

Size: Green iguanas can grow up to 5 to 7 feet long, including their tail. They can weigh between 10 to 20 pounds.

Color: They are usually bright green, but they can also be shades of brown, gray, or even blue, depending on their environment and mood.

WHERE DO THEY LIVE?

Green iguanas are found in the tropical regions of Central and South America. They live in rainforests, near rivers, lakes, and mangrove swamps.
These iguanas are excellent climbers and spend most of their time high up in trees, soaking up the sun.

WHAT DO THEY EAT?

Green iguanas are herbivores, which means they eat plants. Their diet mainly consists of leaves, flowers, and fruits. They especially love leafy greens like dandelion leaves and hibiscus flowers.

SPECIAL ABILITIES :

Tail Whip: Green iguanas have strong, whip-like tails that they can use to defend themselves against predators.

Swimming: They are excellent swimmers and can stay underwater for up to 30 minutes to escape danger.

Color Change: While not as dramatic as a chameleon, green iguanas can change their color slightly to blend in with their surroundings or to show their mood.

FUN FACTS :

Third Eye: Green iguanas have a special "third eye" on top of their head called a parietal eye. It doesn't see like normal eyes but can sense light and movement, helping them detect predators from above.

Communication: They use their body language to communicate with other iguanas. For example, they nod their heads slowly to say "hello" or quickly to show they feel threatened.

Longevity: In the wild, green iguanas can live up to 10 to 15 years, but with proper care, they can live even longer in captivity.

Green iguanas are fascinating reptiles that combine beauty, strength, and agility, making them one of the most intriguing creatures in the rainforest!

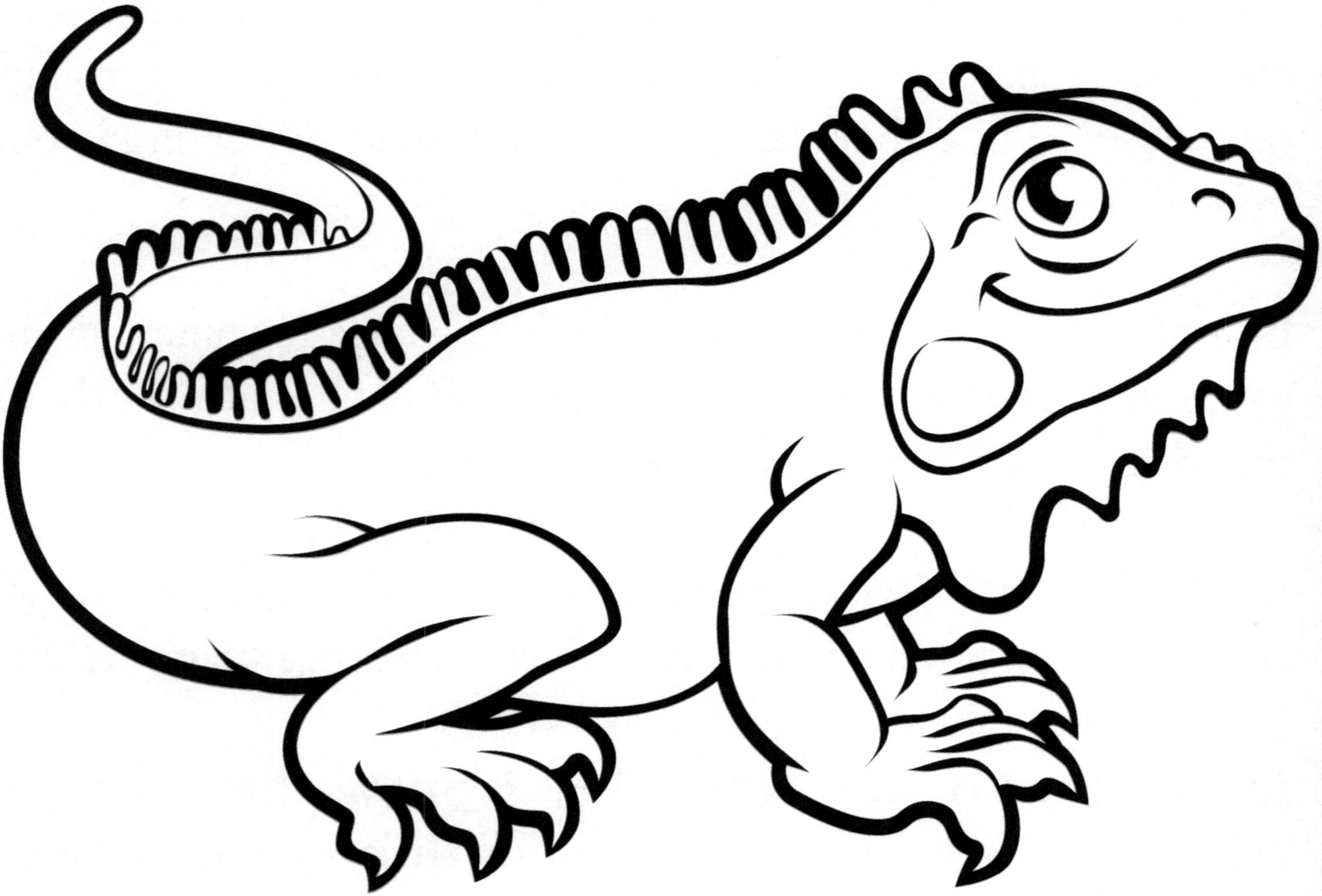

KING COBRA

25.

BASIC CHARACTERISTICS :

Scientific Name: Ophiophagus hannah

Size: King cobras are the longest venomous snakes in the world, growing up to 18 feet (5.5 meters) in length!

Color: They have smooth, shiny scales that are olive-green, brown, or black, with pale yellow bands running down their bodies. Their belly is cream-colored or light yellow.

26.

WHERE DO THEY LIVE?

King cobras are found in forests, grasslands, and swamps throughout Southeast Asia, India, and southern China.
They prefer areas near streams or lakes, where they can hunt and stay hydrated.

WHAT DO THEY EAT?

King cobras are carnivores, and their diet mainly consists of other snakes, including venomous species. They are known for hunting and eating small pythons, rat snakes, and even other cobras.
They will also eat lizards, small mammals, and birds if necessary, but other snakes are their favorite food.

SPECIAL ABILITIES :

Venomous Bite: King cobras have a highly potent venom that can paralyze their prey. Unlike many snakes, they can control the amount of venom they inject depending on the size of their prey.

Hood Display: When threatened, they spread their iconic hood—a wide flap of skin and ribs around their neck—to look larger and more intimidating.

Standing Up: King cobras can lift up to one-third of their body off the ground and stand tall while spreading their hood, which allows them to look humans and larger animals directly in the eyes.

FUN FACTS :

The Snake-Eating Snake: The scientific name *Ophiophagus* means "snake eater," which is fitting for a snake that primarily eats other snakes!

Royal Name: King cobras are called "king" because they can overpower and eat other large venomous snakes, making them the top snake in their habitat.

Nest Builders: Unlike most snakes, female king cobras build nests out of leaves for their eggs and fiercely guard them until they hatch.

King cobras are both feared and admired for their size, intelligence, and powerful venom, making them the true rulers of the snake world!

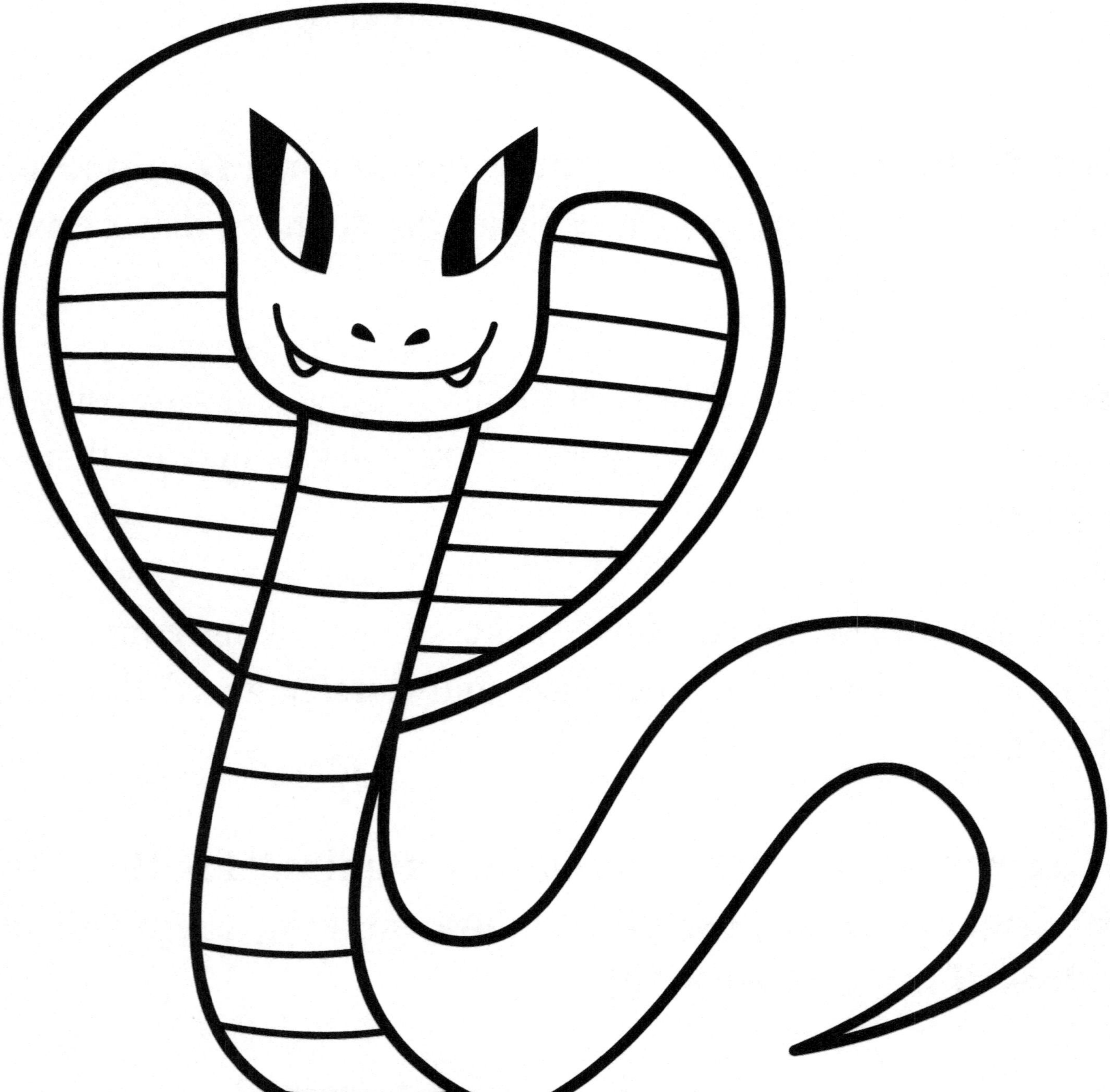

KOMODO DRAGON

BASIC CHARACTERISTICS :

Scientific Name: Varanus komodoensis

Size: Komodo dragons are the largest lizards in the world, growing up to 10 feet (3 meters) in length and weighing over 150 pounds (70 kilograms)!

Color: Their skin is usually grayish-brown with rough, scaly texture and large claws on their feet.

WHERE DO THEY LIVE?

Komodo dragons are native to a few islands in Indonesia, including Komodo, Rinca, Flores, and Gili Motang. These islands are hot, dry, and covered with grassy savannas, forests, and volcanic hills.

They are excellent swimmers and can travel between islands to hunt for food.

WHAT DO THEY EAT?

Komodo dragons are carnivores and top predators in their environment. They mainly eat large animals such as deer, wild boar, and water buffalo. They are also scavengers and will eat **carrion** (dead animals).

Their sharp teeth and strong jaws allow them to rip through flesh, and their saliva contains deadly bacteria and venom that weaken their prey.

SPECIAL ABILITIES :

Venomous Bite: While not as deadly as a snake's bite, the Komodo dragon's saliva contains venom and harmful bacteria. After biting their prey, they track it for hours until it weakens and dies.

Strong Swimmers: Komodo dragons are great swimmers and can dive underwater to catch prey or cool off.

Speed: Despite their large size, they can run up to 12 miles per hour in short bursts to catch prey.

FUN FACTS:

Forked Tongue: Like a snake, Komodo dragons have a forked tongue that they flick out to "smell" the air and locate prey from miles away.

Dragon Babies: Young Komodo dragons spend their early years in trees to avoid being eaten by larger adults. Once they grow big enough, they come down to the ground.

Ancient Relatives: Komodo dragons are often called "living dinosaurs" because they have existed for millions of years and are one of the last large lizard species left on Earth.

Komodo dragons are incredible and fearsome predators, using their size, strength, and intelligence to dominate the islands where they live!

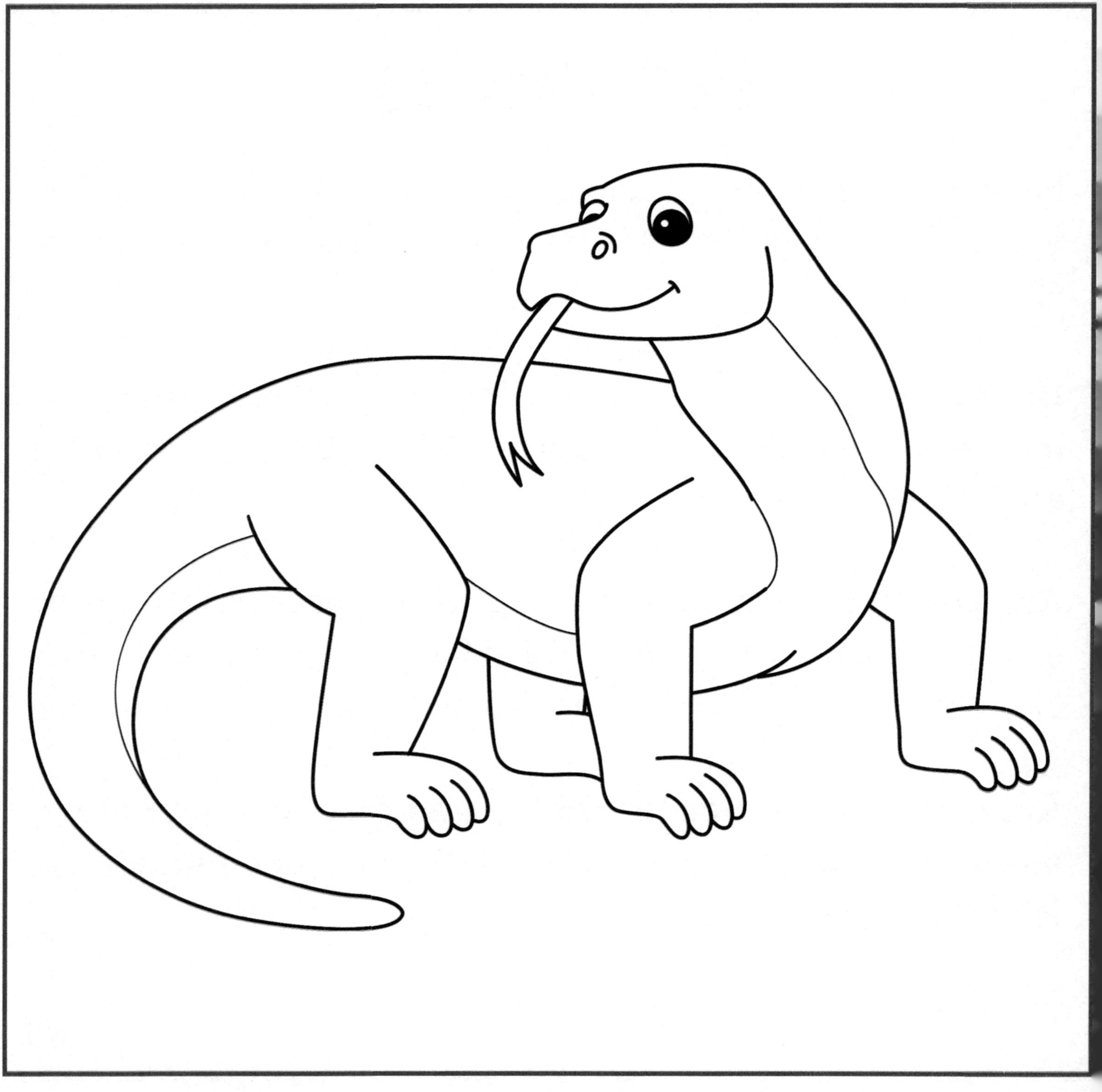

LEOPARD GECKO

37.

BASIC CHARACTERISTICS :

Scientific Name: Eublepharis macularius

Size: Leopard geckos typically grow to about 7 to 10 inches in length, including their tail. They weigh around 50 to 80 grams.

Color: They have yellowish skin covered in dark spots or rosettes, much like a leopard's spots. Some may also have bands or stripes, especially when they're young.

WHERE DO THEY LIVE?

Leopard geckos are native to the dry, rocky deserts of Afghanistan, Pakistan, India, and Iran. They prefer arid environments with sandy soils and rocky outcrops.

Unlike many other geckos, leopard geckos spend most of their time on the ground and are primarily nocturnal, which means they're active at night.

WHAT DO THEY EAT?

Leopard geckos are insectivores, meaning they mainly eat insects. Their diet consists of crickets, mealworms, and other small bugs. In the wild, they might also eat small spiders or scavenge for other tiny creatures they can find.

SPECIAL ABILITIES :

Tail Storage: Leopard geckos store fat in their thick tails, which helps them survive when food is scarce.

Tail Drop: If threatened by a predator, they can drop their tail to escape. The tail will grow back, but it's never quite the same as the original.

Eye Lids: Unlike many other geckos, leopard geckos have movable eyelids, allowing them to blink and close their eyes, which helps protect their eyes from dust and debris.

FUN FACTS :

No Sticky Toes: Leopard geckos don't have the sticky toe pads that other geckos use to climb walls. Instead, they have tiny claws that help them grip the ground.

Quiet Talkers: They can make soft chirping sounds, especially when they're hungry or communicating with other geckos.

Long Life: Leopard geckos can live up to 20 years or more in captivity, making them one of the longest-living lizards you can have as a pet.

Leopard geckos are charming and hardy reptiles, known for their beautiful patterns and gentle nature, making them a favorite among reptile enthusiasts!

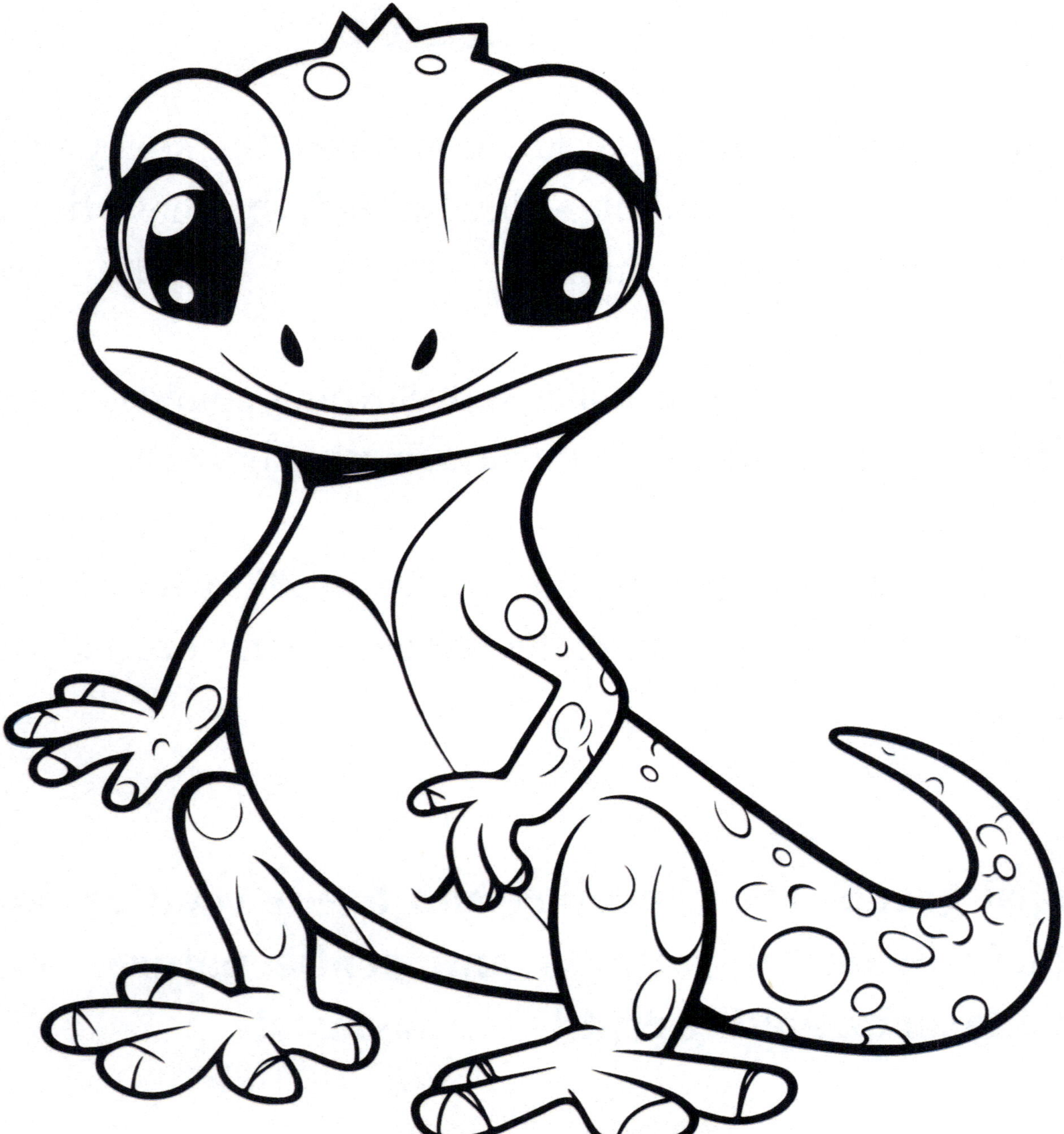

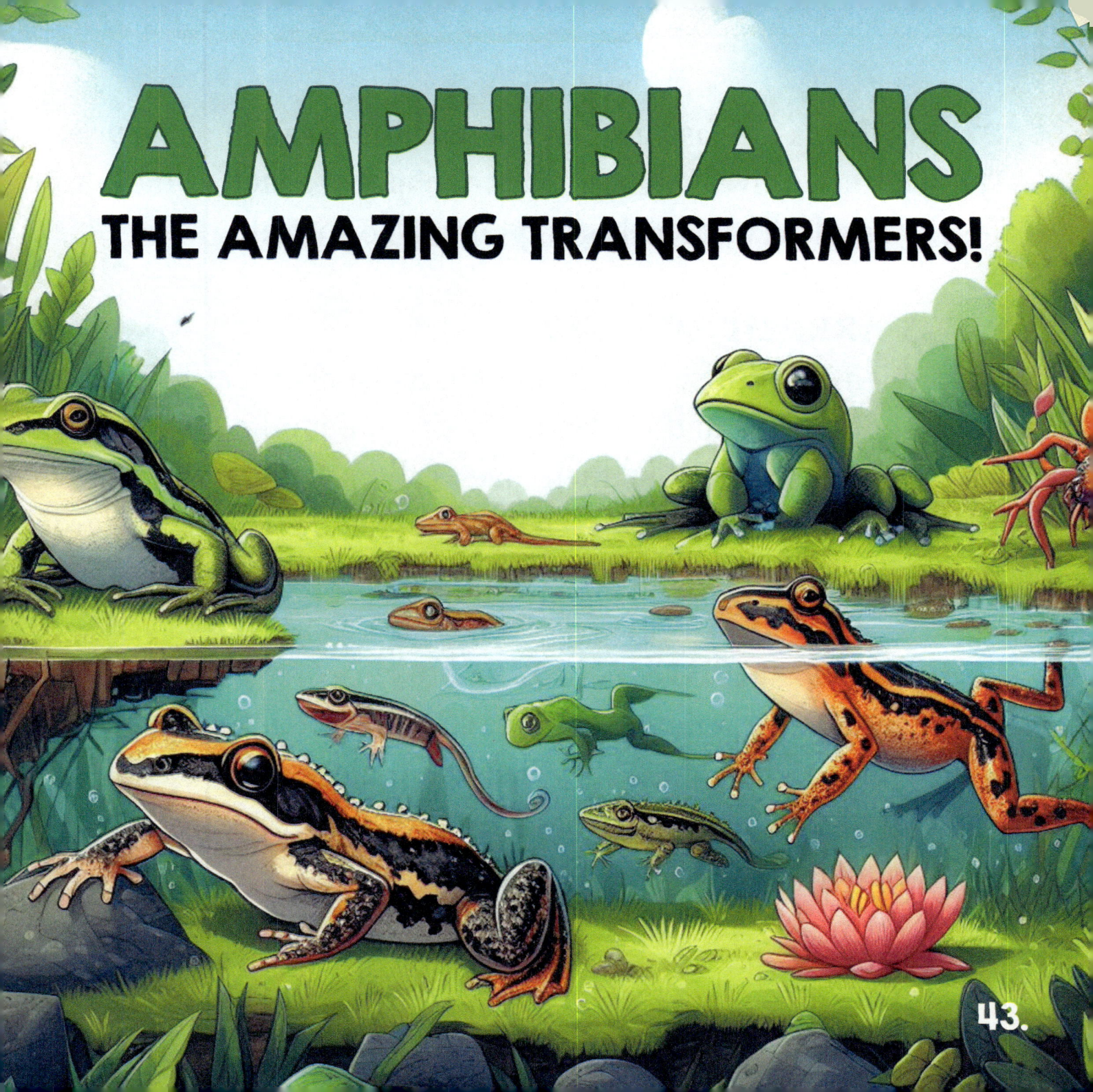

AMPHIBIANS
THE AMAZING TRANSFORMERS!

43.

Amphibians are fascinating creatures that are full of surprises. They start their lives in water and often move to land as they grow up. Let's explore what makes amphibians so special!

WHAT ARE AMPHIBIANS?

Amphibians are animals with smooth, moist skin that helps them live in both water and on land. They're unique because they go through a big change in their lives called metamorphosis. For example, a tiny tadpole, which looks like a little fish, can grow into a hopping frog!

WHERE DO AMPHIBIANS LIVE?

Amphibians need water to survive, so you'll often find them near ponds, lakes, and rivers. They like damp places where their skin won't dry out. Some amphibians live in rainforests, while others can be found in meadows or even backyards.

WHY ARE AMPHIBIANS IMPORTANT?

Amphibians play a big role in keeping nature in balance. They help control insect populations by eating bugs, and they serve as food for other animals like birds and fish. Their sensitive skin also makes them great indicators of how healthy the environment is—if amphibians are thriving, it's a good sign that nature is doing well!

46.

AFRICAN BULLFROG

47.

BASIC CHARACTERISTICS :

Scientific Name: Pyxicephalus adspersus

Size: African bullfrogs are one of the largest frogs in the world, growing up to 9 inches (23 cm) long and weighing over 2 pounds (1 kilogram)!

Color: They have a greenish-brown body with a lighter belly, and males often have a yellow or orange throat.

WHERE DO THEY LIVE?

African bullfrogs are found in sub-Saharan Africa, in countries like South Africa, Namibia, and Botswana. They live in grassy savannas, wetlands, and near water sources such as ponds and rivers.

They spend much of their time buried underground during the dry season, waiting for the rains to come.

WHAT DO THEY EAT?

African bullfrogs are carnivores with a huge appetite. They eat insects, small mammals, birds, and even other frogs. Anything that can fit into their big mouth might become their next meal!

They also have sharp teeth called **odontoids** on their lower jaw, which help them hold onto their prey.

SPECIAL ABILITIES :

Burrowing: During the dry season, African bullfrogs burrow underground and form a protective cocoon out of their own skin to stay moist and survive until the rainy season returns.

Powerful Jumps: Despite their heavy bodies, they can leap long distances to catch prey or escape predators.

Vocal Calls: Males are known for their deep, booming calls, which they use to attract mates and establish territory during the rainy season.

FUN FACTS :

Super Dads: Male African bullfrogs guard their eggs and tadpoles fiercely. If the water where the tadpoles live starts to dry up, the father will dig a channel to help them reach deeper water.

Survival Experts: They can go without food for months while buried underground, living off the energy stored in their body.

Long Lifespan: African bullfrogs can live up to 20 years in the wild and even longer in captivity.

African bullfrogs are tough, resourceful, and powerful amphibians that can handle Africa's extreme seasons, making them one of the most fascinating frogs in the world!

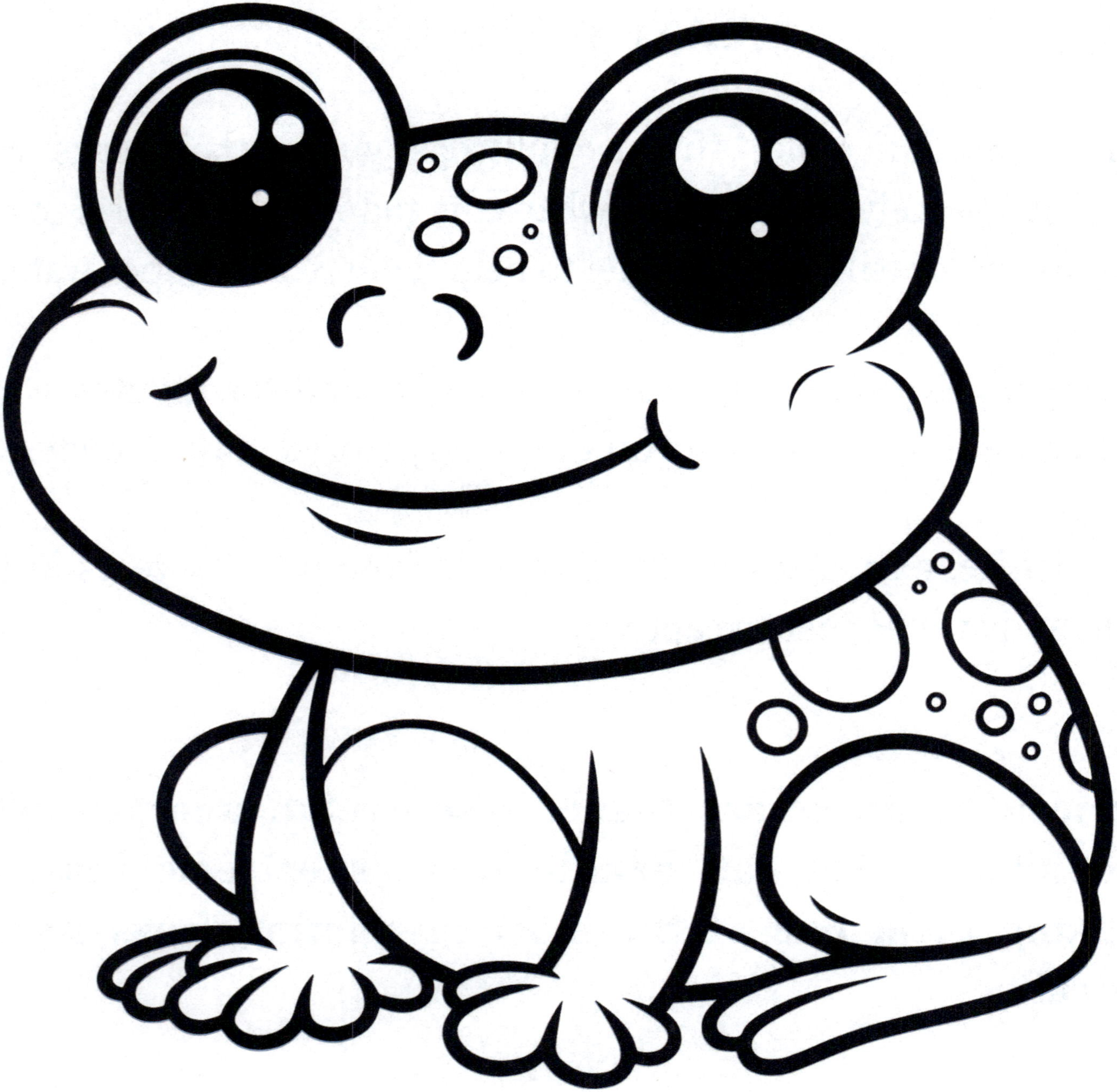

AXOLOTL

53.

BASIC CHARACTERISTICS :

Scientific Name: Ambystoma mexicanum

Size: Axolotls grow to about 6 to 12 inches (15 to 30 cm) long, with most being around 9 inches (23 cm).

Color: They can be pink, white, brown, or black. Axolotls often have a cute "smiling" face due to the shape of their mouths and wide heads.

54.

WHERE DO THEY LIVE?

Axolotls are native to the freshwater lakes and canals around Mexico City, specifically Lake Xochimilco.
Unlike most amphibians, axolotls spend their entire lives underwater and rarely venture onto land.

WHAT DO THEY EAT?

Axolotls are carnivores and mainly eat small aquatic creatures like worms, insects, and tiny fish. In captivity, they often eat bloodworms and special pellets.
They use a suction-like motion to gobble up their prey, pulling it into their mouths.

SPECIAL ABILITIES :

Regeneration: One of the most amazing things about axolotls is their ability to regrow lost body parts! If they lose a limb, tail, or even part of their heart or brain, they can regenerate it completely within a few weeks.

Breathing Underwater : Axolotls have external gills that look like feathery branches on the sides of their heads, which help them breathe underwater. They can also absorb oxygen through their skin.

FUN FACTS :

Endangered: Wild axolotls are critically endangered due to pollution and habitat loss. However, they are popular pets and widely studied in labs because of their regeneration abilities.

Friendly Faces: Axolotls have a permanently "smiling" expression, which makes them very popular among pet owners.

Unusual Relatives: Axolotls are related to tiger salamanders, but they never leave the water like their relatives do.

Axolotls are fascinating creatures with unique features that make them unlike any other amphibian, from their permanent larval stage to their incredible regenerative powers!

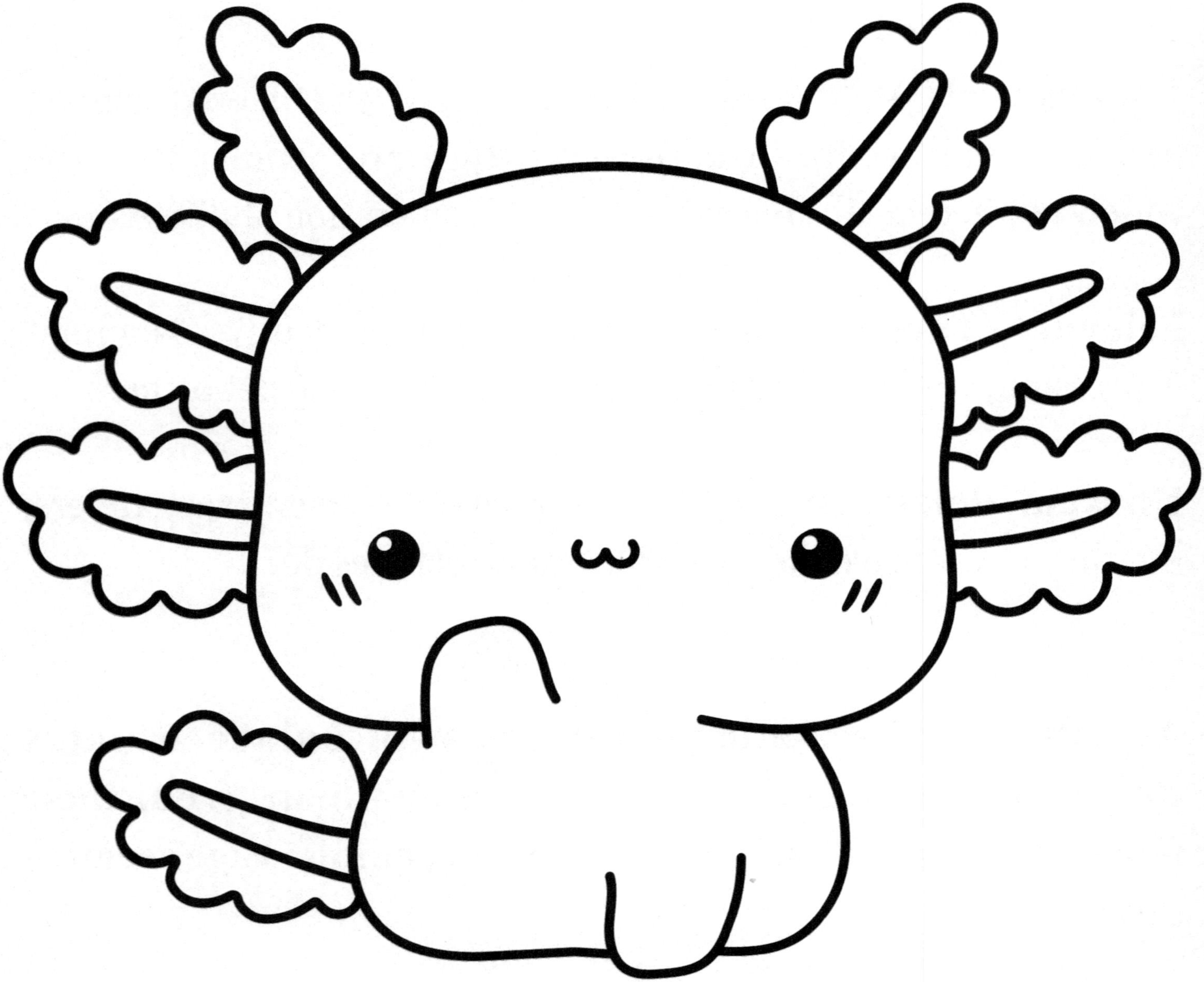

POISON DART FROG

BASIC CHARACTERISTICS :

Scientific Name: Dendrobatidae

Size: Poison dart frogs are small, usually growing to around 1 to 2 inches (2.5 to 5 cm) long.

Color: These frogs come in bright, vibrant colors like blue, yellow, green, orange, and red, often with striking patterns of spots or stripes.

WHERE DO THEY LIVE?

Poison dart frogs are found in the rainforests of Central and South America, particularly in countries like Costa Rica, Brazil, and Colombia.

They live in humid environments near streams, ponds, and rivers, where they spend most of their time on the forest floor or climbing trees.

WHAT DO THEY EAT?

Poison dart frogs are insectivores, meaning they eat small insects like ants, termites, and beetles.

Their diet in the wild is what gives them their toxic skin—certain insects they consume contain toxins that the frogs absorb and store.

SPECIAL ABILITIES :

Toxic Skin: Poison dart frogs produce a powerful toxin through their skin. In some species, this toxin is so strong it can be lethal to predators and even humans. Indigenous people in South America used the frog's toxins to coat the tips of blow darts for hunting, giving the frogs their name.

Bright Warning Colors: Their bright colors are a warning to predators that they are poisonous. This is called *aposematic* coloration, which helps them avoid being eaten.

FUN FACTS :

Safe in Captivity: Poison dart frogs raised in captivity are not poisonous because they don't eat the toxic insects found in their natural habitat.

Parenting Frogs: Many species of poison dart frogs are caring parents. Some carry their tadpoles on their backs and deposit them in small pools of water in plants called ***bromeliads***, where they continue to protect them.

Tiny but Mighty: The golden poison dart frog, one of the most toxic species, has enough poison to harm or even kill several humans, making it one of the most dangerous animals on Earth!

Poison dart frogs may be small, but their dazzling colors and powerful toxins make them stand out as some of the most fascinating amphibians in the rainforest!

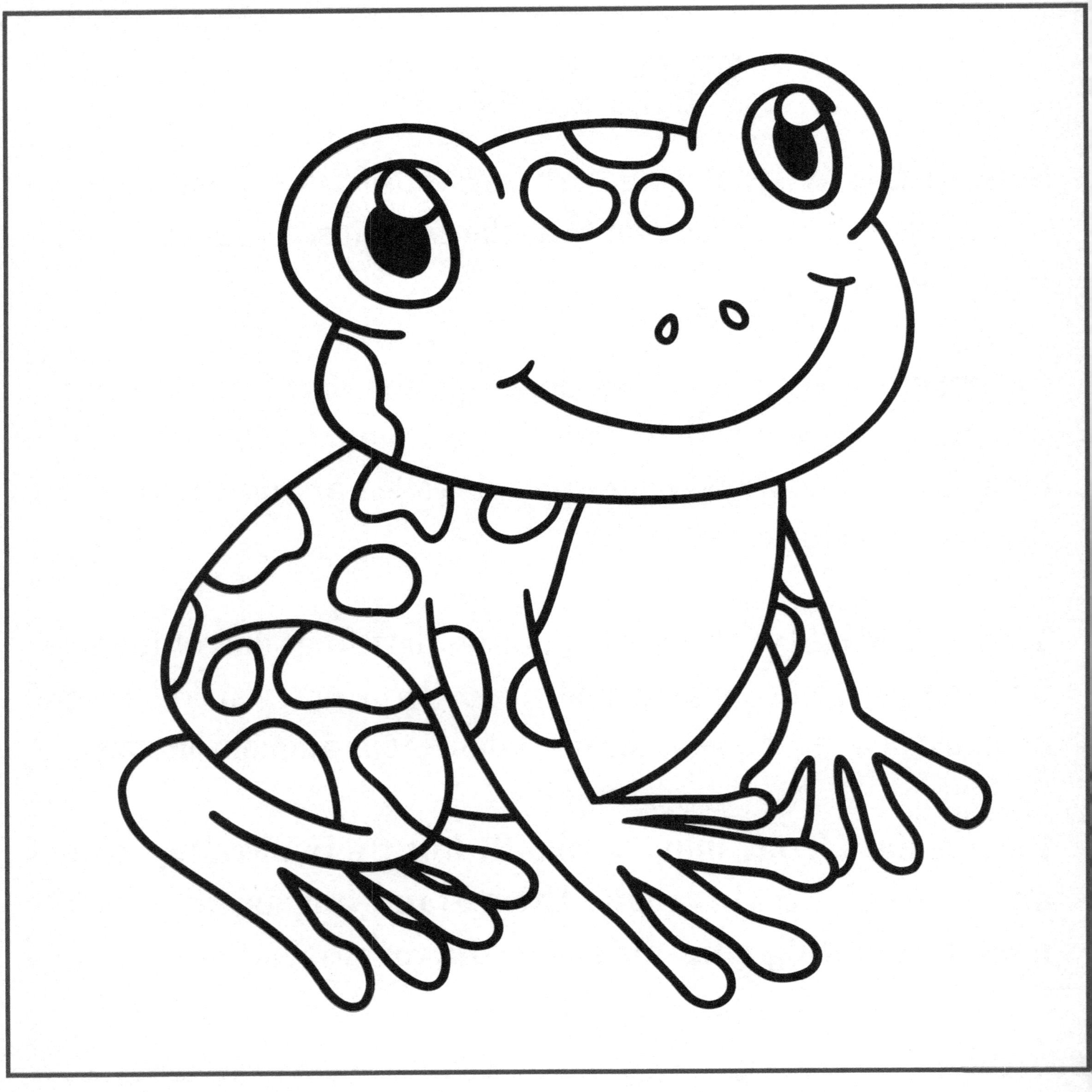

RED-EYED TREE FROG

65.

BASIC CHARACTERISTICS :

Scientific Name: Agalychnis callidryas

Size: Red-eyed tree frogs are medium-sized frogs, growing to about 2 to 3 inches (5 to 7.5 cm) long.

Color: They are known for their bright green bodies, striking red eyes, and blue and yellow stripes on their sides. They also have orange toes that help them grip tree branches.

66.

WHERE DO THEY LIVE?

Red-eyed tree frogs are native to tropical rainforests in Central America, including countries like Costa Rica, Panama, and Nicaragua.

These frogs live in trees near ponds, rivers, and other water sources, where the humidity helps keep their skin moist.

WHAT DO THEY EAT?

Red-eyed tree frogs are carnivores and mostly eat insects, like crickets, flies, and moths. They may also eat smaller frogs or invertebrates like spiders.

They use their long, sticky tongues to quickly snatch up prey.

SPECIAL ABILITIES :

Camouflage: During the day, red-eyed tree frogs hide their bright colors by tucking in their legs and closing their eyes. This helps them blend into the green leaves they rest on, making them nearly invisible to predators.

Startling Eyes: When threatened, they pop open their bright red eyes and flash their colorful legs to scare off predators. This defense tactic is known as "startle coloration."

FUN FACTS :

Egg Guardians: Red-eyed tree frogs lay their eggs on leaves hanging over water. When the tadpoles hatch, they drop into the water below, where they continue to develop.

Bright Colors: Although their vibrant colors may seem dangerous, red-eyed tree frogs are not poisonous. They rely on their camouflage and jumping abilities to stay safe.

Night Creatures: These frogs are nocturnal, meaning they're most active at night when they hunt for food and avoid predators.

Red-eyed tree frogs are one of the most visually stunning frogs in the animal kingdom, known for their bold colors and remarkable jumping skills!

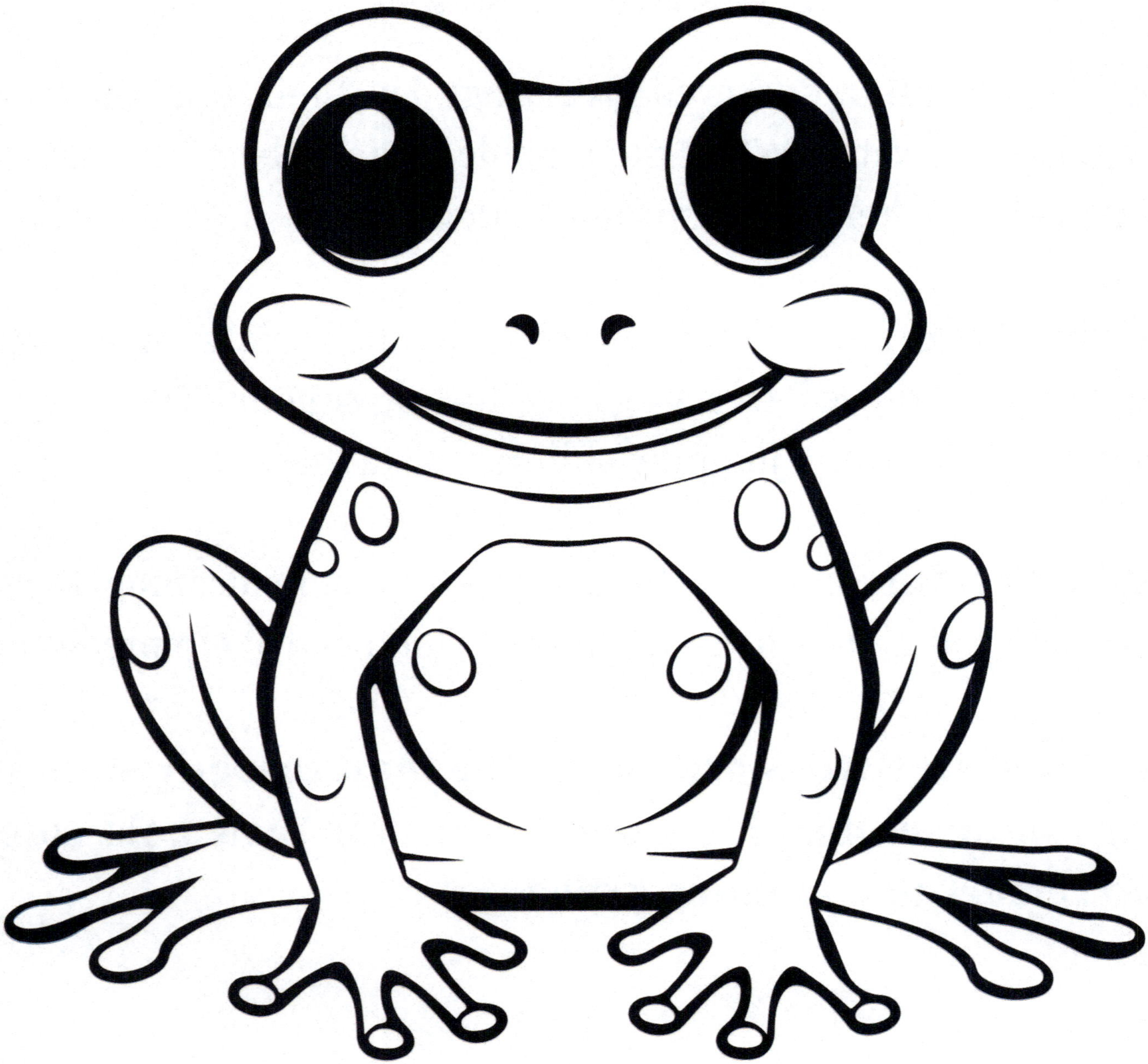

TIGER SALAMANDER

BASIC CHARACTERISTICS :

Scientific Name: Ambystoma tigrinum

Size: Tiger salamanders are one of the largest salamanders in North America, growing up to 6 to 14 inches (15 to 35 cm) long.

Color: They have dark, black or brown bodies with bright yellow or greenish stripes or blotches, which make them look like little tigers—hence their name!

72.

WHERE DO THEY LIVE?

Tiger salamanders are found throughout North America, in a variety of habitats including forests, grasslands, and marshes. They like to live near water sources like ponds and streams but spend most of their time on land.

These salamanders are excellent burrowers and often dig underground to hide from predators or find cool, moist areas to stay hydrated.

WHAT DO THEY EAT?

Tiger salamanders are carnivores and have a big appetite! They eat insects, worms, slugs, and small invertebrates. They are also known to eat small frogs and baby mice.

They are ambush predators, waiting quietly for their prey to come close before snapping it up with their strong jaws.

SPECIAL ABILITIES :

Burrowing: Tiger salamanders are powerful diggers. They can burrow deep underground to escape dry or cold weather, keeping them safe and cool.

Regeneration: Like many amphibians, tiger salamanders can regenerate parts of their body, including lost limbs, tails, and even parts of their eyes!

Larval Life: Some tiger salamanders stay in their aquatic larval form for their entire lives, like axolotls, never fully developing into land-dwelling adults. This is called *neoteny*.

FUN FACTS :

Long Lifespan: Tiger salamanders can live up to 20 years in the wild, which is very long for an amphibian.

Secretive: They are rarely seen because they spend most of their lives hidden underground or in burrows, only coming out during rainy nights or breeding season.

Toxic Skin: Like many amphibians, tiger salamanders can secrete mild toxins from their skin to deter predators, though they are not dangerous to humans.

The tiger salamander is a fascinating and secretive amphibian, known for its bold stripes, underground lifestyle, and amazing ability to regenerate lost body parts!

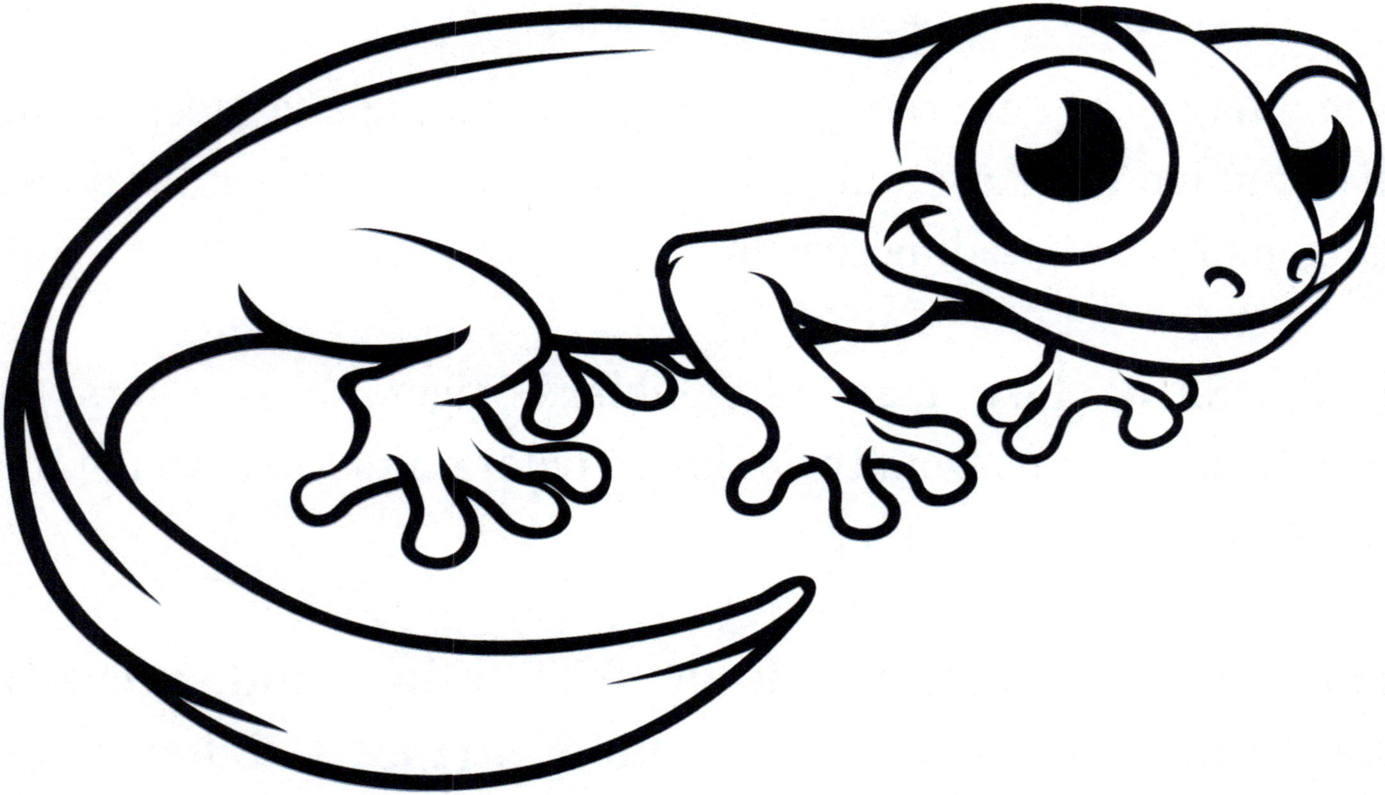

TIPS AND TEACHINGS :

CARING FOR REPTILES AND AMPHIBIANS

🍃 RESPECT WILDLIFE: 🍃

Both reptiles and amphibians are important parts of nature. They help keep ecosystems balanced by controlling pest populations and serving as food for other animals. Always observe them from a distance and avoid touching or disturbing them in the wild.

🍃 PROTECT THEIR HOMES: 🍃

Reptiles and amphibians live in forests, deserts, ponds, rivers, and wetlands. Help protect their habitats by not littering, avoiding pollution, and picking up trash when you visit these natural places. Keeping their environments clean ensures they have safe homes.

🍃 BE GENTLE WITH PETS: 🍃

If you have reptiles or amphibians as pets, make sure to care for them properly. Research their needs, such as the right temperature, clean water, and specific food. Never release pet reptiles or amphibians into the wild, as this can harm local ecosystems.

🍃 CONSERVATION IS KEY: 🍃

Many reptiles and amphibians, like the Galápagos tortoise or axolotl, are endangered due to habitat destruction and pollution. Learn how conservation efforts protect these amazing creatures and how you can help by supporting wildlife preservation programs.

🍃 LEARN BEFORE YOU INTERACT: 🍃

Some reptiles, like snakes or lizards, and certain amphibians, like frogs and salamanders, can be delicate or even dangerous if handled incorrectly. Always ask an adult before interacting with any wild animals and remember to keep them safe by not disturbing their natural behaviors.

🍃 WATER MATTERS: 🍃

Amphibians need clean water to survive, and reptiles need access to safe habitats. You can make a difference by conserving water at home and supporting efforts to keep rivers, lakes, and wetlands clean.

DEAR YOUNG EXPLORERS,

At **RainbowInk Press**, we believe that every adventure into the natural world is a chance to learn and grow. As you explore the incredible reptiles and amphibians featured in this book, remember that each creature plays a special role in our world. By respecting their habitats, protecting their homes, and learning about their amazing abilities, you become a part of their story.

We hope this book inspires you to cherish the wonders of nature and take small steps to help keep our planet beautiful and safe for all its inhabitants. Thank you for joining us on this journey of discovery!

Happy Exploring,

RAINBOWINK PRESS